Ten Minutes' Peace

An Oasis for Moms

Susan McGrath

PublishAmerica
Baltimore

First printing

At the specific preference of the author, PublishAmerica allowed this work to remain exactly as the author intended, verbatim, without editorial input.

ISBN: 1-4241-2045-4
PUBLISHED BY PUBLISHAMERICA, LLLP
www.publishamerica.com
Baltimore

Printed in the United States of America

For Lincoln and Sawyer,
who occasionally allow me eight or nine minutes.

To Tim—P.S.

Thanks to the Lord for letting me use my writing to bless others; my parents for everything, especially computer time; my mother-in-law for her prayers and appreciation; Jeff Garrison for giving me a forum and helping me find my audience; Bill Thomas for encouragement in all things; Marilyn Kater and Sue Ade for still believing in me even though I'm not anchoring the national news; Nancy Smart for having a voracious appetite for words; Cheri Wysong for teaching me it's okay to make a mess when you're having fun; the Cole family who inspired many of these ponderings; the kids in my youth group for keeping me from getting old; kindergartners everywhere for being themselves; and my small group "family" for being there.

Devotions for All Seasons

"A Bible and Mr. Bubble"

The other day I found myself in another conversation about childbirth. As moms we love to compare and scare with our horror stories of labor and delivery. (And ours is always the most horrible!) Don't we love to ask that first-time mom, "How long was *your* labor?," knowing that no matter what her answer is, we have a story to top it?

The truth is that for most moms the labor is eighteen years and counting! We never stop worrying, encouraging, feeling guilty, and loving. And stay-at-home moms can honestly tell people they have the best job in the world.

Having been on both sides of the time clock, I know it is satisfying to be home with that toddler learning to talk—and frustrating to go an entire day without speaking any word over two syllables! Let's face facts: Raising children is joyful, depressing, hilarious, rewarding and exhausting—and that's just before lunch!

Some days it's hard to remember the feel of a bubble bath or the taste of a lunch that doesn't include peanut butter or hot dogs. Those are the times we really need that ten minutes of peace (and locking ourselves in the bathroom doesn't count)! The Lord has many encouragements for mothers, especially on the importance of our "job." Take that ten minutes and splash around in Psalms or have a refreshing taste of Proverbs and I promise you will be uplifted!

All moms are full-time moms, but some are blessed not to have to put on any other hats. Regardless, we know that the "Mom" hat with its sticky fingerprints and smudges of who-knows-what is the most important one we will ever wear. At least we *need* to know it, and to acknowledge and encourage it among each other, because the world won't.

After all, Proverbs 22:6 says, *"Train a child in the way he should go and when he is old he will not turn from it."*

How's that for a challenging job?

"I Am a Mother"

I am a mother. Period. No justification. No add-ons, so that I appear to be an uninteresting underachiever. No excuses for why I have a family and want to take care of them. Just "I am a mother."

I have participated in God's miracle of birth. I have been given the honor of acting as care giver and protector of a helpless, innocent child.

I have been kissed by long lashes and sticky lips. I have played hide and seek, Hi Ho! Cherry-O and Candyland more times than I can count.

I have watched Barney videos until I sing the songs in my sleep. I have eaten at McDonald's an average of once a week.

I have had my toes trampled by little feet and my heart trampled by little words.

I have prayed over each child as they lay sleeping. I have dreamed of what they will turn out to be.

I have sung lullabies and patted backs, bandaged scraped parts and hauled others to the emergency room to be "glued."

I have fixed three different menus for the same meal. And I have said, "You can eat what I fixed or find your own supper."

I have struggled through homework and delighted in learning to read all over again from a six-year-old's perspective.

I have complained to my family and friends about my children, and I have cried for fear that I am not doing a good job.

I have yelled and then felt bad all day, and I have praised and hoped it meant something to my child.

I have just begun to understand what I put my mother through.

I believe we are sometimes afraid to put motherhood forth as the most important thing we do, even if we believe it is! The most difficult and important job we will ever have is raising children to know the Lord and be an asset to His kingdom.

I have worried over the enormity of this task. I have prayed about it. I have worried some more.

I am a mother.

Let's strive to be like the mother in Proverbs 31 and Timothy's mother and grandmother, Eunice and Lois (2 Timothy 1:5). Let's give our worry and our children over to the Lord and seek to be the mothers God intended.

"Beauty for Ashes"

I love winter and snow. I have joked with my husband about moving to northern Minnesota! Many people hate the cold, the mess, the inconvenience of winter weather, but I have always seen it as beautiful and refreshing.

About three years ago we had a few inches of snow topped by some freezing rain. As I got up that morning I noticed how beautiful the pine trees in the neighbor's yard looked as the sun shone on the ice. It was a magical winter wonderland.

But about two hours later I got a phone call from my father. He asked if I was sitting down, and told me that a young mother in our church had been killed in a car accident. She had skidded on the ice on her way to work.

The beauty of the day was replaced by horror. I couldn't believe something so beautiful could be so deadly. That morning my son and her youngest son were attending the same preschool class. I couldn't imagine someone having to pick up a four-year-old and tell him he no longer had a mother. I couldn't imagine the teacher being able to continue with class after hearing the news.

Though the snow and ice no longer looked beautiful that day, God's beauty was evident in the weeks to come as her family and the community tried to adjust.

Praise God that what comes from Him is always beautiful! We

don't have to worry that it will turn to dust, that it will cause harm. In fact, when we have ugly or unbearable things in our lives, he will replace them with His beauty.

As Isaiah 61 says, the Lord will give us *"beauty for ashes, gladness instead of mourning, the mantle of praise instead of a fainting spirit."*

Does that mean we will never have tragedy in our lives? No. But our loving Father provides us with something to overcome any obstacle—joy, peace and grace.

As we enjoy the beauty in our world, let's remember the true beauty is not what God allows us to see with our eyes, but what we experience through His love.

"Got Joy?"

The advertising world seems to be overly concerned about what we carry around with us. The famous American Express credit card commercial has featured many celebrities who say they "don't leave home without it!" A more recent credit card ad campaign asks, "What's in your wallet?"

We do worry a lot about how much money we carry around, or whether we have packed everything in the diaper bag or our favorite shade of lip gloss in the make-up case. But how often do we think about what we're carrying on the inside? And how much of it shows through to the outside?

A wonderful Christian lady I met through our youth programs gave her daughter the name Carrie Joy, because she wanted her to always "carry joy."

I thought that was a wonderful gift to give a child.

It's a wonderful gift we can give to God, ourselves and others as well. If we carry joy, it doesn't mean we have to be happy and bubbly twenty-four/seven. It just means we have a deep and peaceful understanding of God's love and we know He can bring us through anything. That is true joy.

Some of my favorite praise choruses and hymns are about joy.

There are over 225 bible verses about joy. (Not including the "joyful" and "joyous" ones.)

This week let's find our joy and hold onto it with at least one hand as we navigate the day, and just maybe some of it will be spread to others.

Rather than listing *my* favorite lyrics and verses on joy, I challenge you to take ten minutes this week to write down some of your favorite songs or choruses about joy. Sing them—in the shower or anywhere, even if you get funny looks from your kids! Then see if you can find the scripture they are based on.

Happy, happy joy hunting!

"Enjoying the Moments"

As I worked on the computer one evening my youngest son, at the time two years old, was busy creating a work of his own.

I didn't hear a sound (which should have tipped me off right away), but when I came through the kitchen to search for him—there he was in front of an open cabinet putting the crowning touch on a tower of food to rival any toddler-engineered project in history!

The foundation consisted of cans of green beans and tomatoes, upper stories featured a jar of peanut butter and containers of lemonade. Precariously perched on top was a gleaming *glass* bottle of taco sauce.

A horrible vision of collapse and a red, spicy layer spattered over the kitchen flashed through my head.

I shifted into preventative mode and gently moved my son away while praising him for constructing such a marvelous monument.

Just to clarify—our son did possess a few toys, among them Lego's, Duplo blocks, wooden blocks, cardboard alphabet blocks, stacking cups and some others I can't think of at the moment. So why would he rather stack vegetables when he has a roomful of bright-colored, mind-stimulating toys?

Who can fathom what goes on in the brain of a two-year-old?

This is the kind of thing I used to get really uptight about. My mouth would logically and loudly explain that we "don't do things like that," while my hands would turn compulsive and hurriedly put everything back into its proper place.

Now instead, I called my husband in to see what our "little genius" had built and grabbed a camera to preserve his masterpiece for years to come.

I still strive for the patience I need in many situations. I don't always stop and enjoy all the little moments that I should or could, but God has extended his grace to me in all that I do. He has blessed me in so many ways. Surely I can show some to others and be an example to my children of God's love.

"...put your hope in God, who richly provides us with everything for our enjoyment."—1 Timothy 6:18 (paraphrased)

"What's Love Got to Do with It?"

You know it's nearly here when hearts and roses are everywhere. Chocolate is prominently displayed at Wal-Mart. Most of the men you encounter are trying to ignore the signs or pretend they don't know what month it is.

For some of us Valentine's Day means romance and roses. For others, disappointment or disgust as the day is ignored by a spouse. For moms of grade school kids it might mean plowing through the class list as your child painstakingly writes each name on a Valentine. For a friend of mine who delivers wholesale roses by day and helps run a home-based chocolate business in the evenings, it means chaos and exhaustion!

But what does love have to do with a holiday that is named after an ancient "saint" and drowning in commercialism? Hallmark, Hershey and FTD will all tell you their product is the best way to show your love this year. Granted, for some of us chocolate does equal love, but that's another page!

What does God have to say about love? As far as I know chocolate is not found in the bible. (I'm still searching!) But love is mentioned a *few* times.

We are told that God shows his love for us in this: while we were yet sinners, he sent his son to die for us. This is the love that is most important to Christians, as it means grace, salvation and eternal life with God. It is the love we need to share with others so they can know Him.

But how do we express that love? How do we live it? Scripture also tells us, "Greater love has no man than this, that he lay down his life for his friend." That's certainly a hard one to live up to.

What about 1 Corinthians 13, "the love chapter":

Love is patient—yet I berate my husband when he doesn't clean out the basement or gather up the tax information as quickly as I want him to.

Love is kind—yet I yell at the kids when they mess up the house and beg for everything in the store, because I've had a bad day dealing with critical people.

Love does not envy—yet I am jealous to the point of anger that my neighbor gets to be a full-time stay-at-home mom and drive a new van, while I work two part-time jobs and drive something ten years old.

Love is not self-seeking—yet I pout and whine until I get my way, or my husband's attention, when I feel he has neglected me because of a busy week at work.

Love is not easily angered—yet I use words like "stupid" and "lousy" to describe the driver who just cut me off, as my kids listen in the back seat.

Love keeps no record of wrongs—yet I remember how that woman at church criticized my child's behavior when her child is certainly no angel, and I know exactly which years my husband forgot Valentine's Day.

I have to confess I have been guilty of most of these loveless acts a one time or another. So I pray this scripture, that I might remember what love is.

Love does not delight in evil, but rejoices in the truth—so I will stand up for God and godly events and organizations in my community and school.

Love always protects—so I will be an encourager to those I love and anyone around me who needs some extra kindness.

Love always trusts—so I will put my faith in God and ask for guidance in doing His will and I will be open and loving with my spouse.

Love always hopes—so I will keep my eyes fixed on Christ and remember what I have to look forward to someday, regardless of how badly my day has gone.

Love always perseveres—so I will continue to pray for the lost around me and the seemingly hopeless situations. I will share Christ with those who want to hear and those who don't.

Love never fails. God never fails. Therefore, God = Love. In this instance, the equation works! This week, read 1 Corinthians 13 and plug in your own personal experiences regarding the qualities of love. And buy yourself a box of chocolates!

Happy Valentine's Day!

"Pass the Vitamins"

The church across the street from my congregation once had this bit of wisdom on their sign out front: "The most important vitamin for a Christian is B1."

If we are to "be one," a Christian that is, don't we need to be giving others a boost with an encouraging word via our favorite medium (A note sent through the postal service is fine for those who are technologically challenged, or whose mothers raised them to write letters like proper ladies).

I can think of several times when I have felt really low and overwhelmed by all my obligations and projects, and a note of encouragement has come from someone at just the right moment.

One Sunday a woman in our congregation came up to me and said she really appreciated that I had written her a thank-you note, because many people don't bother to write them anymore. (My mama raised me right!) She said it had really encouraged her that morning.

I was a bit puzzled, since I couldn't remember writing anything recently. I asked her what it was about. It turned out to be a note I wrote to her almost a year before, yet that day it had appeared in her mailbox at church. We never did figure out where it had been all that time. (God's ways are higher!)

The way we receive encouragement at the time when we most need it should make us take notice of how God works and how much He cares for us!

The most encouraging note I think I ever received was a sympathy card when my grandfather died. The reason it meant so much was not what it said, but because of who it was from and when it was sent. The woman who sent it to me had lost her daughter in a car accident the previous year. She must have mailed my card on or very near the anniversary of her daughter's death. But rather than dwelling on her loss, she chose to bless me!

I believe God constantly provides us with opportunities to bless others—we have to choose to make use of them and allow Christ to shine through us.

Each morning as we take our vitamins (and girls, make sure yours have iron and calcium supplements), let's ask God to show us how to "boost" and bless someone else.

"Give, and it will be given to you. A good measure, pressed down, shaken together and running over, will be poured into your lap. For with the measure you use, it will be measured to you."—Luke 6:38

“A Good Read”

I love a good read!

News articles, magazine features, romance or historical novels, biographies, self-improvement, humor, history—I will read about most any topic if the information is well crafted.

I read many different genres, viewpoints and styles. When I love something, I want to read it again, although not without some time to savor the delicious taste it left me with. When it’s well written and has drawn me into the story, I never want it to end. I also love to recommend it to my friends.

But I’m sure you’ve read books that made you wish the author had told the story in fewer words. Instead they went on and on and on…

But the Bible isn’t like that. It is God’s infallible, perfect word.

Certain parts may seem to us to be full of unnecessary details, or leave out the details we want to know. Sometimes we have to dig deeper. These are words inspired by God and they either tell us what was or is, or they provide a parable or illustration to help us understand a truth or event.

God didn’t want us to wade through a swamp of unfamiliar or convoluted words. He conveyed only information that is useful. We can either apply it, relate it or learn from it. It contains commands, expectations, parables, historical biographies, and regional customs as well as prophecies and promises.

The Bible holds everything we need to know—who God is, what He did for us, what He expects of us and how it should all be accomplished.

As a writer, I know how hard it is to crank out a few coherent, cohesive paragraphs on a weekly basis. I can't imagine trying to coordinate and edit a project that took scores of authors and hundreds of years to put together, had no contradictions and appealed to every culture throughout history!

(That's why God is God and I'm a small-time columnist!)

"Voices Carry"

The house where I lived as a child was built in 1921 and owned and occupied by only one family before my parents bought it in the early 1970's. Many remnants of the original owners' lives remained tucked in corners and cupboards. One of my favorites as a child was a large floor radio from the 1930's.

It stood in the upstairs hallway and many times when my mother was ensconced in her sewing corner, or on a rainy afternoon, my brother and I would visit distant places via this mysterious, tube-filled antique cabinet.

The reason it was so fascinating was not that it contained pre-set buttons for major stations in our area, like WGN, WMAQ or KMOX (kings of the Midwest airwaves in the early twentieth century), or that it was as big as we were. The thing we thought was so cool was the variety of "bands" or channels it displayed, which included "Police" and "Overseas."

I don't remember that we ever had much luck with the police band, but the overseas was amazing to two grade school kids—like the worldwide web of the 1970's!

It even listed exotic places we could tune to: Central America, Brazil, London, Paris, Rome, Japan. We delighted in turning through the languages we couldn't understand, trying to identify what they might be. It seemed like a direct connection to a huge, exciting world.

I hate to give away my age, but this was almost thirty years ago.

There were no twenty-four hour news channels, no foreign language channels. We didn't even know anyone who spoke another language except for a couple of missionaries who came home on furlough and visited our church every couple of years.

What a different planet it is today! Over the last three decades the world has drawn closer together, from satellites to CNN, cell phones to surfing (with a keyboard rather than a surfboard).

I don't remember the last time I tried out the old radio. I thought it would be neat to show my kids when they were old enough to play with it, but somehow I don't think they would be as impressed with it as I was.

Our world has come together on an information level, but not on many other levels. I guess communication is a place to start, anyway. It's also a place to start with God. He hears all our voices, whatever the language or need. The closer we are to him, the better and clearer our communication will be.

When we have a personal relationship with the Lord and support that through prayer, scripture study and fellowship we will not only be able to "hear" what the Lord wants, but understand. The language of his will can become our native language.

Isn't it wonderful that we have an open line to the Lord any time? We don't have to waste time scanning for the right station or getting rid of static. We don't have to worry how many minutes we have left or wait until the weekend to connect.

Our voices carry clearly to God no matter where or when. And his blessings carry back to us!

"And pray in the Spirit on all occasions with all kinds of prayers and requests. With this in mind, be alert and always keep on praying for all the saints."—Ephesians 6:18

During your ten minutes' peace this week, thank God for the opportunity and power of prayer.

"Who Do You Know?"

Watching a televised funeral for a U.S. Senator who spent almost 50 years in office, through the terms of ten different presidents, I thought about how many important people he knew in his lifetime.

There were probably many "ordinary" people who wanted to meet or get to know this man—he had connections, influence, power, wealth to some extent. All this could put someone on the path to a great career or successful business.

Who wouldn't want the opportunity to be in his inner circle. Most of us are impressed by, or would like to experience for a short time, what a position like that brings.

Though celebrities may not push our buttons, what about those with popularity or authority in our community or church? How often have we seen people go out of their way to impress the preacher?

Yet what can any of these people do for us? Perhaps make us feel important or give us some advantage in this world. But Paul wrote as he was imprisoned for sharing the gospel, *"That is why I am suffering as I am. Yet I am not ashamed, because I know whom I have believed, and am convinced that he is able to guard what I have entrusted to him for that day."—2 Timothy 1:12*

Wow! That's something even a United States senator or president can't provide.

It's easy to forget that who and what we know is not as important as who and what we are. As Christians we are part of a large body of believers and ambassadors for Christ to those around us.

When we leave this life, as the senator did, it will not matter what former or current presidents speak at our funerals. It will not matter how many people read our books or if our names and faces were recognized by the world. In fact, it will only matter that we knew one person—Jesus Christ, and that we introduced others to Him because of who He is! I love the T-shirt that says "It's who you know that determines where you go!" That may be true to some extent in life on earth, but it is unquestionably true for eternity! Let's remember to focus every day on our relationship with the only one who will make a difference eternally.

"I want to know Christ and the power of his resurrection and the fellowship of sharing in his sufferings, becoming like him in his death, and so somehow, to attain to the resurrection from the dead."—Philippians 3:10-11

"Wallowing"

Do you ever just want to roll around in it?

That self-pity, discontent, anger and indignation?

It's been one of those weeks! Your children are the worst-behaved on the block (or in Sunday school), your husband discovered termites in the family room and you can't find the library books that were due two days ago! Though not earth-shattering, these irritations on top of all the everyday stresses and imagined failures just make you want to yell and whine a little, "It's not fair! Why don't my kids listen to me? Why won't my husband (fill in the blank)? Why can't I have at least one good hair day this week?"

My grandfather was a pig farmer (in addition to corn and beans). When I was very young, I remember thinking it was fun to "help" him feed the pigs. I also remember wanting to hold and pet the cute, pink, clean baby pigs. Did I mention they were clean? Usually still in the farrowing house stall with their mama. And clean!

I had no desire to be near the large hogs who rolled around in the odorous mud. In fact, I'm sure I turned up my nose at them.

That's probably what people want to do to me when I wallow. Although it feels good for the moment, as the cool mud does to the pigs, it quickly loses its appeal and gives off a stench that is offensive to everyone in close proximity.

When I wallow, I know I'm denying God the chance to comfort

and teach me, to help me grow spiritually. Sometimes I even pull others down to roll around in the mud with me. Kind of a group wallow.

God gives us the alternative to "wallowing" in 2 Corinthians 4. It's even been put to music, a little praise chorus called "Trading My Sorrows." It says, "I'm trading my sorrows, I'm trading my shame, I'm laying them down for the joy of the Lord." Then from 2 Corinthians 4:8, *"I am pressed but not crushed; persecuted, not abandoned; struck down but not destroyed."* God is bigger than all our troubles and He will hose off the mud and provide us with hip boots if that's what it takes.

So my prayer when I feel like wallowing will be, "Lord, when the rains fall, help me to stay out of the mud!"

"Cloud of Sin"

The Gospels tell us that in the hours before Jesus' death, as he hung on the cross in agony, darkness came over the whole land—the sun stopped shining—for about three hours in the middle of the day!

Isn't that spooky? I've read several explanations from scientists: It was a total solar eclipse. It was a cloud of volcanic ash which traveled from an eruption thousands of miles away. (This, by the way, also explained the earthquakes at the time of Jesus' death.)

Now, if God wanted to make it dark by using his natural resources, he certainly could. But I don't personally believe that's how it happened. It think however he did it, it represented what his son was suffering. It was the black stain of all the sins of everyone from the beginning of time, pouring down onto one man hanging on a cross.

We have seen the physical suffering of Christ portrayed graphically on the big screen. But I think that was nothing compared with the emotional and mental anguish he suffered as he was crushed down by all the horrible things his creation had done and would do.

Christ did that for me. God allowed his son to shed his precious lifeblood for someone completely undeserving. I guess that makes me someone special.

As you reflect on the cross this week, think of what Jesus did for you personally. Thank him and remember that what he went through paid everyone's admission to heaven. We just have to let them know which flight to catch!

"Precisely"

In "The Lord of the Rings: The Fellowship of the Ring" (movie version, not the book) when the wizard Gandalf arrives in the Shire, he is greeted by his friend Frodo Baggins, who simply says, "You're late."

Gandalf looks at him with a bit of a scowl and says, "Wizards are neither late, nor are they early—they arrive *precisely* when they mean to!"

It reminds me of Christ's arrival. The Jews, who as God's chosen people had been anticipating the Messiah for hundreds of years, may have felt he was a little late. Perhaps that's why so many chose not to accept Him.

Mary, who had no idea of her part in God's plan to save the universe until about nine months before it came to be, and was an unmarried virgin, may not have been quite ready.

But God was. Precisely.

Webster's defines "precisely" as: *exactly or sharply defined or stated; minutely exact; or distinguished from every other.* I love that last definition! How perfectly it describes the Messiah!

God had given the message to many prophets for hundreds of years. He had described the place and manner in which this miracle would occur. Months before it happened he prepared Mary for the shock of her life, then calmed Joseph's concerns. Precisely.

God prompted the most powerful man on earth at the time to call for a census of his vast lands, requiring Joseph to travel with Mary to his hometown, the city of David, from whence prophets said the Messiah would come. God made sure His son was born where He said he would be.

Precisely.

God continued to orchestrate these details throughout the life of His son on earth. Up to and including his painful death and his glorious resurrection.

Details like the type of wounds Christ would endure. Isaiah speaks of Him being pierced and crushed—the crown of thorns and the beating, or perhaps even the lung-crushing torture of hanging on the cross, and His burial with the rich – a wealthy member of the Jewish Sanhedrin, Joseph of Arimathea, who donated his own tomb.

Precisely.

God fulfilled all the hundreds of prophecies made about the Messiah through Christ in the flesh.

Precisely.

When I have a concern, large or small, where should I go?

Precisely!

"Traffic Jam"

All of us at one time or another have been in a traffic jam, whether rush hour on the freeway or fighting our way out of a parking garage after watching our favorite team win.

Traffic jams are usually to be found in a metro area or, in the case of my small town, after a sports or school event. There are times after ball games in our little hamlet when a police officer has had to direct traffic from the school, and it still takes twenty minutes to thin out the cars.

Over a two-year period, two new church buildings were built across the street from my home church. Both are well-attended and have many active ministries.

Although our schedules are not identical, there are Sundays when I have left morning worship and had to wait several minutes to pull out onto the street because of cars leaving the other two parking lots.

Once I had to wait over three minutes—a long time for a residential street in my town. It was almost like a school or sports event! In fact, it occurred to me that if the traffic got much more congested, we would need to call in a traffic cop.

I realize that for many large congregations this is already a real concern, but wouldn't it be wonderful if the general population were so eager to worship and know the Lord that church parking lots overflowed and traffic lights had to be activated for Sunday mornings?

What if we showed such love and reached out to so many that dismissal of our worship service looked like fans streaming out of a major league ballpark? (All the time—not just for concerts or Vacation Bible School or old home week!)

Not that any of us enjoy being stuck in traffic, but if this were a major problem faced by congregations everywhere, wouldn't we shout, "Hallelujah!"?

Or would we complain that "it's too crowded" and "we don't know all these people" and "things aren't like they used to be," and "we'll never get to the restaurant before those people from the church down the block," and on and on?

Hmm...I wonder why we don't have more traffic jams after church?

Matthew 28:19 says, *"Therefore go and make disciples of all nations, baptizing them in the name of the Father and of the Son and of the Holy Spirit, and teaching them to obey everything I have commanded you."* (All nations would include our nation, our city, our neighborhood.)

As you find your ten minutes' peace this week, pray for revival in your congregation and community. Ask God to show you how to reach out to those who need to know Him and where you can minister best in your church.

"Are You Listening?"

When my youngest son was about twenty months old he climbed on the couch one day and began running back and forth, a stunt he often tried to get away with. I told him, "No. Get down before you fall." But he grinned and kept running, and before I was able to remove him from the situation, he bounced off and fell to the floor. His ego was much more bruised than he was, and as I said, this was not his first experience with bouncing off furniture.

I picked him up and tried to explain again in toddler terms that jumping on the couch is not a smart thing to do. Before I was finished talking he was trying to go at it again.

It made me think about how I don't always listen to God. Sometimes I'm in a situation I know could turn out badly and I feel the Spirit prompting me to act in a certain way. But I've already made my decision to do things *my way*. Then even when I fall on my face, I may go the wrong direction again because I'm sure I can find a better way to accomplish what *I* want.

God must be the most frustrated parent ever! We think having one child who is particularly strong-willed, or even one who won't listen to us as we try to sneak past the toy aisles at Wal-Mart, is extremely embarrassing, and makes us feel like a failure.

Think how many of us at any given moment are ignoring God's nudge toward wisdom or even screaming in rebellion for everyone to hear.

Proverbs 1:5 tells us, *"let the wise listen and add to their learning, and let the discerning get guidance."*

James also has important words on this subject. He says, *"Everyone should be quick to listen, slow to speak and slow to become angry."* He follows in verse 22 with, *"Do not merely listen to the word and so deceive yourselves. Do what it says."*

Perhaps that is where we can learn from our children. Have you even had one of your kids look up at you wide-eyed as you carefully explain something, then watched that child turn around and do the complete opposite?

How often do we do that to God? By being better children to our Heavenly Father, we will surely learn to be better parents.

"Pleasing Aromas"

The scent of fallen leaves in autumn, freshly bathed babies, funnel cakes at the fair, old houses in the spring, a real Christmas tree, pot roast as you walk in the door on Sunday after a long sermon, new cars, leather, new cars with leather interiors, lemons, Play-Doh, raindrops on roses (and whiskers on kittens—sorry, I got carried away!)—most of us would agree these are lovely aromas.

I know smells or aromas can be more nostalgic for me than almost any sight or sound. I've read that women are very sensitive to aromas and link them closely with memories. It's true for me!

I grew up in a large old house with plaster walls and lots of woodwork. As the weather would warm up in the spring the house seemed to breathe and the aroma is not something I can describe, but if you've ever experienced it you know what I mean. It's not quite old wood mixed with fresh air, but close.

My husband and I purchased our own old house (even older than my parents' home) and I've noticed it has that same aroma. It's not as prevalent—maybe because my house has been partly renovated, contaminated with drywall—but when I climb the stairs, I can catch a whiff of it near the top.

It's a comforting aroma. Most people might not even notice it, but for me it smells like home.

Paul tells the Corinthians, *"We are to God the aroma of Christ among those who are being saved and those who are perishing. To the one we are the smell of death; to the other the fragrance of life." (2 Corinthians 2:15-16)*

This means just as everyone isn't captivated by the aroma of old homes, everyone won't receive God's message from us with a big smile. Some will, though, and since we don't know which are which until we share, we must always wear our "aroma" and embrace those who embrace the gospel.

As a familiar aroma is a comfort to us, something to evoke pleasant memories, or the signature of a place of refuge, we must be those things to our brothers and sisters in Christ and to those who are seeking to understand the message of Christ. We must strive to bring out those feelings of warmth, coming home, belonging.

At the end of verse 16 Paul asks, *"And who is equal to such a task?"* It does sound like a big responsibility! But he answers in the next chapter. *"Not that we are competent in ourselves to claim anything for ourselves, but our competence comes from God. he has made us competent as ministers of a new covenant—not of the letter, but of the Spirit..." (2 Corinthians 3:5-6)*

God provides the aroma. All we have to do is put it on!

During your ten minutes this week, think of your favorite aromas and praise God for the memories and the people linked to them. Then ask him to help you be the aroma of Christ!

"Coincidence or Providence?"

In the movie "Signs" Mel Gibson's character asks, "What if there are no coincidences?"

(If you don't remember the line or haven't seen the movie, it doesn't matter. That was just my clever segue into this topic!)

There's also a saying that coincidences are just miracles we don't give God credit for.

Perhaps both are true. I'm sure you've all had many experiences which, upon later reflection, seem a little too convenient. Things just worked out too perfectly not to have been guided by someone.

I want to share an incident that happened in our community.

It was Fire Safety Week, and the elementary school where I was working and which my son attended was having its first fire drill of the school year. But this year, instead of going to the fence at the edge of the property, each class crossed the street at the nearest corner and waited on the sidewalk, a safety measure to get everyone farther from the building.

I only worked at school in the mornings, so after lunch I made a few necessary stops around town—Wal-Mart for diapers, the post office, etc.—then went to school to pick up my son.

I arrived a little early so I parked across the street to wait for dismissal time. Just as I picked up something to read, I noticed kids beginning to stream out of the building from every door. I couldn't believe they were having a second fire drill. It seemed like overkill. (I was just glad I wasn't in charge of prodding the kindergartners out the door this time.)

Then, just as the last class came out the back door I heard a huge BOOM! I knew immediately what it was. It had the distinct sound of a gas explosion and they had been working on the furnace all week, and were still working when I left just two hours before. I thanked God that someone had been alerted in time to get everyone out!

As they lined up on the sidewalk next to my car I was asked to help sort the kids into bus lines and get them to parents, since no one could go back into the building. While shuttling kids across the street and anxiously watching the firefighters and emergency workers checking the building, I was told that a technician working on the furnace was the only one injured—and it was minor!

Also, that the principal hadn't been aware of the problem with the furnace boiler. He had scheduled a second fire drill for that exact time.

Coincidence or providence?

Is there a difference? I'll let you ponder all the "what if's" of this potential tragedy. God has a purpose and plan for us. We will never know all the times we may have come this close to disaster. God is good.

This week during your 10 minutes, search out some verses on how God guards and cares for us—even when we are blissfully unaware.

"Return Label"

A kindergarten teacher I work with makes a scrapbook for each of her students at the end of the school year.

Included among "letters to mom," hand prints, drawings and achievements is a class picture with this message,"I am returning your child to you after nine months of learning—a couple inches taller, a few pounds heavier, more confident and prepared for his next step in life."

It goes on to say that after so much time together, they will always be a part of each other and if someday, years from now, they meet on the street, they will both smile and get a twinkle in their eyes. Then she thanks the parents for the privilege of teaching their child.

I wonder what the label on my children will look like when they are grown and I let them go out into the world?

Perhaps something like this:

"God, I am returning this child to your care. Though he is really no longer a child, I hope he will look to you as his Father. He is a different person from the squirming, squalling infant who was placed in my arms years ago.

I tried to teach him right from wrong from the time he was a toddler, and "please" and "thank you" before he headed off to preschool. I have laughed and cried with him, for him and because of him through painful childhood lessons and teenage heartaches.

Through it all I prayed, and probably preached, about the need to trust and follow you. I took him to church and chaperoned the youth outings. I read my bible where he could see it and sent him to church camp.

I explained over and over why he couldn't when his friends could. I asked for you to help me be a better mom. I hope he thinks I was and knows that I tried my best.

I told him I loved him.

God, you know my prayers and love will never stop. I will always worry some and maybe even meddle a little. Help him to feel my love and yours.

I am returning him to you to continue to grow, to change the world for you, to someday do the same for his children."

With Inexpressible Gratitude,

A Mother

Happy Mother's Day!

"To the Garden"

In my kitchen hangs an antique picture titled "The Little Gardener." My great-grandfather won it as a prize for selling garden seed over one hundred years ago when he was just seven or eight years old.

I had never noticed it in Granddad's home. But after he died, my grandfather brought it to his home and hung it in the family room. From that time on I always told him how much I loved the picture and that I would like to have it someday.

I've never learned anymore about it. The frame is likely as old as the picture, the glass wavy. It shows a young boy wearing overalls and a straw hat, holding a shovel. A small wooden wheelbarrow nearby holds flowers ready to plant. It evokes precious memories of my great-grandfather, who wore a similar hat when he worked outside or went fishing, and my grandfather, who always wore overalls for farming and gardening. Both loved to work the earth and were both masters at it.

When you hail from a long line of farmers and gardeners, it's supposed to be in the blood. But I'm not much of a gardener. I don't like bugs. I don't like heat and humidity. I don't like my back to hurt. I do love fresh vegetables and flowers. As long as someone else grows them. I'll help pick and freeze the vegetables, cut and arrange the flowers, even get my hands dirty planting. Just don't ask me to get anything to grow. I'm content with the results of someone else's work.

Sadly, this is too often true in our spiritual lives. We are content to let someone else do the planting (sharing the Word) and even the growing (making disciples), and, hey, spill some of that fruit this way if you don't mind!

God is the Master Gardener. He gives us the ability to grow and the assorted tools we need to nurture others. Just as many gardeners have their specialty—whether watermelon or prize roses—God has many types of fields for us to work and a variety of souls to be harvested.

1 Corinthians 3:5-9 tells us, "*—as the Lord has assigned to each his task. I planted the seed, Apollos watered it, but God made it grow. So neither he who plants nor he who waters is anything, but only God who makes things grow. The man who plants and the man who waters have one purpose, and each will be rewarded according to his own labor. For we are God's fellow workers; you are God's field, God's building.*"

So as you work your garden this season, or enjoy the fruits of someone else's garden, reflect on the garden of souls around you and ask God which soil is fertile for planting and who needs water.

To the garden!

"Mine"

My son has a book that I love reading to him called *Mine!* It's about a little girl who never wants to share her toys.

A friend comes over to play, and with each toy her friend picks up she yells, "Mine!" and takes it away. Mom intervenes and suggests they play with her new tricycle. They take it to the park and the little girl rides for awhile. But when her friend wants a turn she yanks it away and yells, "Mine!" The tricycle flies out of her hand and rolls down a hill, bouncing and banging along the way, losing parts left and right.

When they all reach what's left of the tricycle at the bottom of the hill the friend looks at it and says, "Yours!" and walks away.

I know my kids can be selfish and thoughtless when it comes to what they think belongs to them. Maybe you can relate.

But what happens when we, as mature adults and hopefully growing Christians, feel ourselves falling into the "mine" trap. It may not be over "toys" or even our tithes and offerings to the Lord. We may neglect to pray over a tough decision, thinking we know best and don't need God's counsel. Maybe when it comes to our children (they're definitely ours, right?) we are the final authority on what is best.

Well, God has a few things to say about what belongs to whom:

Revelation 7:10—*"Salvation belongs to our God..."*

Ezekiel 18:4—*"Every living soul belongs to me..."*
Job 41:11—*"Everything under heaven belongs to me..."*
Psalms 111:10—*"To him belongs eternal praise."*
Job 12:13—*"To God belong wisdom and power."*
Job 12:16—*"To him belong strength and victory..."*

However, God also promises that some things belong to us:

1 John 2:25—*"This is what he promised us—even eternal life."*
Romans 5:1—*"We have peace with God through our Lord Jesus Christ."*
Matthew 11:28—*"Come to me, all you who are weary and burdened, and I will give you rest."*

God makes it easy on us. He takes care of most everything if we remember it is His to begin with. Take time this week to give back to God what is His, not just in service and finances, but control in all areas of your life.

"Summer Sanity"

Popsicles sticking. Swimsuits dripping. Skin burning. Mosquitoes biting. Kids whining: "I'm bored." "It's too hot." "It's raining! What can I do now?"

Lawn mowing. Picture taking. Book reading. Late sleeping. Flowers growing. Watermelon eating. Lightning bug catching.

The mess. The itching. The tedium. The delights.

Why such a mixture of dread and high expectations for summer? We've grown up knowing through songs, poems and the advertising industry that it is to be a restful, even "lazy," time. With no school and little work we can sit back and sip lemonade, enjoying life as it happens.

Except it rarely happens that way! We have just as many schedules to balance (if not more) than during the school year. Sports, camps, summer art and reading programs, Vacation Bible School and daily clamoring from those adorable children to swim, take a bike ride or play with friends.

So how are we to find serenity in this "lazy" time of year, or even keep our sanity?

Start by remembering that God created this season. God created your family. He has a plan for them during this time—even if you don't! God doesn't put us in a triathlon without good running shoes, fully-aired bicycle tires, goggles and sun screen. If the lemons are abundant in our summer, God will provide the sugar to sweeten them or at least some iced tea to help wash them down.

We need to trust the Lord, then we need to focus on making any extra time with our kids productive. Get them to church camp. Even if they are away from us for a few days, the experience will be life-enhancing and we'll have much to discuss when they get home with their dirty clothes and sticky luggage!

Don't forget about Vacation Bible School. If your church doesn't have one, there's probably one in your community that does. This is a great time for your kids to invite friends who don't know the Lord and also a great time for fellowship. You can always use your talents to serve by helping out with the VBS program.

Take a family trip. This doesn't have to be a budget-busting deluxe vacation. It can mean a day trip to hike in a state park or visit to a free museum. Just something out of the ordinary you can do as a family. (Whatever fits the budget.)

Read. Let the kids choose favorite bible stories. (They can read them to you if they're able.) Visit the library. Dust off that bookshelf and read some favorite stories you all love. Write your own stories and tell or read them to each other. (Who knows, you may get a best-seller out of it!)

Use this time to get to know your kids and make sure they know who the Lord is and see him in us!

"He decreed statutes for Jacob and established the law in Israel, which he commanded our forefathers to teach their children, so the next generation would know them, even the children yet to be born, and they in turn would tell their children. Then they would put their trust in God and would not forget his deeds but would keep his commands."—Psalms 78:5-7

As you find your ten minutes' peace with the Lord this week (and all summer), remember to take ten minutes for your family as well.

"Foreign Diplomat"

I traveled with youth from my church to a convention in Chicago one summer. The group we were with provided all kinds of helpful information to help us save money. One of the top things on the list was to bring the tax exemption number from the church and be approved to use it.

So I dug through some files the night before, came up with the documentation and was all prepared. (The hotel had suggested this to our organization, by the way.) We took an early train (like the sun was still asleep) and arrived about 10 am., well before check-in time. (Which the hotel also recommended we do, as the larger rooms would be given out on a first-come, first-served basis.)

After winding my way through the rope maze, I proceeded to the hospitality clerk, gave my name and presented my tax exemption documentation, to which she replied "Oh, we only honor that for foreign diplomats."

Now, aside from being on the edge of frustration, my mind was also processing the ridiculousness of that statement. Foreign diplomats are exempt from everything in this country, the least of which includes taxes.

I'd only had three hours sleep the night before and a quick doze on the train, so my wit was not at its sharpest. A couple hours later while taking a relaxing tour I thought of the come-back: "Ma'am, I am a citizen of heaven and an ambassador for Christ, so surely that qualifies me as a foreign diplomat."

Well, I was given plenty of opportunity to act out that claim. My patience continued to be tested that day. The desk clerk took our cell phone numbers and told us to check back in an hour if they hadn't called that our rooms were ready. We arrived back at the hotel two hours later and checked to see if our room was ready. It wasn't. We window shopped and had a snack and wondered where our luggage was and talked with arriving friends (some of whom were given a room immediately) and checked on our room again. It wasn't ready.(Keep in mind that this is a famous luxury hotel.)

By the way, did I mention that our room wasn't ready yet?

I was supposed to help register others in our organization as they arrived, so with no room in which to repair my sleepy, train-rumpled look, I proceeded to my post. But I sent one of the kids to check, and guess what? They said the room was ready! Except she couldn't get the keys because her name wasn't on the room list. So I went to my first meeting and then headed down to get my room keys before the next session began.

And would you believe it—our room WASN'T ready! They couldn't explain to me how it got un-ready during that hour, but ready it was not! (The very polite gentleman at the desk asked housekeeping to put it on the priority list.)

I would just like to have been on the list that some of our friends apparently got on when they arrived at 3 p.m. and were handed a key.

So I went to my second meeting—late. When it was finally over, and my eyes and brain were both swimming from exhaustion and I wasn't sure whether to scream or cry, I was able, for the sixth time, to wait in line to see if my room was really ready.

It wasn't! But housekeeping would send someone to inspect it. At this point I decided to express my frustration (After all, a large sign at the desk said to let them know if they were less than perfect. Gee, I wonder if this situation qualified?)

I told the guy I felt I should be compensated and asked for a free night. (We were staying four.) He said he could give me half a night. But not in cash, as my check had already been processed. How about some gift certificates to our hotel restaurant? (Somebody knows how to keep the profits in the building.)

Sure, why not? Just give me some keys!

"Oh, and by the way," he informed me, "that big room with two bathrooms that the clerk promised you when you registered at ten this morning...we gave it to someone else. But here's a smaller one for you." (Okay, he didn't say it like that, but that's how I heard it!)

I'm happy to report, though, that at 8 p.m., only ten hours after checking in, we finally got a room! The bellman who brought up our bags said he thought that was a record wait—at least for the day!

So how did I do as an ambassador for Christ? I didn't yell at anyone, or even treat them rudely. But I sure thought about it. Perhaps instead of a sightseeing tour, I should have had a prayer meeting.

"We are therefore Christ's ambassadors, as though God were making his appeal through us. We implore you on Christ's behalf: Be reconciled to God."—2 Corinthians 5:20

"Protective Arms"

I saw a couple on a talk show once who purified the air and water in their home to give their two-year-old daughter "the best start" she could have. They also refused to immunize her and would not allow her to eat any animal products (dairy or meat).

The mother had never been away from her for more than two hours at a time and even the grandparents had not been allowed to watch her until she was well past a year old because something might happen to her. She was still nursing and was sleeping with mom while dad slept on the couch, because that was best for her development.

Their intentions were to protect her from any toxin in the air or food supply and make her feel safe. They even went beyond that, giving her classes in sign language, music and foreign languages to nurture her intellect.

(It was way too intense for me!)

After I managed to get my jaw off the floor, I wondered if they were as concerned for her spiritual well-being. Did they have her in a bible class? Did she attend Sunday school?

As parents we all have a protective instinct toward our children and a unique way of parenting them. The goal is to give our kids the best start they can possibly have.

We should be just as concerned with babes in Christ. Many are children who were brought up in church and make a decision to commit their lives to Christ. Other are adults when they make that decision, so they don't need much guidance, right?

What if everyone who came out of the baptistry was enfolded not just in a soft warm robe, but protective arms, encouraging words and firm hands to guide them in the path of righteousness?

We are to bring the lost to Christ, but we are also to make sure they stay found.

In John 21, Jesus tells Peter, "Take care of my sheep" and "Feed my lambs." He wants those who know Him to continue to learn and grow in spirit. Paul reminds us throughout the New Testament to encourage one another.

In 1 Corinthians 13:7 Paul says "Love always protects...." We know that we are to have love for each other—so wrap someone in your protective, loving arms this week and show them Christ.

"A Business Bath"

When my brothers and I were young we loved to take long baths, bring in all the toys and run the tub full of water. But once in awhile, like after a long day or on a Saturday night when Mom was preparing stuff for Sunday dinner and Dad needed to prepare his Sunday school lesson we were ordered to take a "business bath."

I thought this was a punishment listed in the parent handbook, but apparently *my* parents made it up. I know this because when my oldest son was about three I told him he was going to have a business bath and explained what that meant—take care of the business of getting clean—no toys, no extra time, no extra water! When my husband overheard me. He laughed.

"A business bath! What's that? Did you make that up?"

I replied, "No! Didn't you ever have to take a business bath?"

At which point he launched into a lie about his deprived childhood and how they had to share the same bath water. Yeah, right!

Anyway, I now punish my kids when I'm too tired for the strung-out, full-tub, 27-toy bath by saying, "Tonight we're having a business bath!"

This is met with much moaning and whining, quickly followed by begging to read longer since the baths will be short.

I believe worship can be like a spiritual bath. We pour ourselves out, we pray for a renewed spirit. But sometimes I think worship is relegated to a "business bath" level. We show up and include all the required elements, then move on the rest of the day and something that will be more fun.

How sad! I know this does not apply to all people or all congregations, but most of us have been guilty of going through the motions of worship. The songs didn't move me that day. The sound system squealed. The kids behind me whispered or rattled papers or dropped things. Someone played music too loud during the Lord's Supper. No one played any music during the Lord's Supper. The auditorium was too hot. The sermon didn't seem to apply to me. I had to serve up front, in back or in the nursery so I couldn't get into the proper frame of mind.

Worship is one of the few things we can offer God—He already has it all! Sometimes I am ashamed when I get distracted by one of the things listed above, or begin to think about the afternoon or next week or anything other than God as I "worship." I need to be focused—and not in a stoic, solemn way that lacks joy. I need to come before the Lord with gladness and pour myself out through praise, scripture reading, prayer and meditation. I need to listen to His words spoken and take them in and allow Him to bless me.

Just as kids love to splash around in a full tub and take their time getting clean, so should I splash around in songs of praise and scripture and enjoy a time of renewal and fellowship!

"Worship the Lord with gladness; come before him with joyful songs."—Psalms 100:2

“Boundaries”

Two houses up the street from us lived two little girls near the ages of my two boys. They enjoyed playing together outside and riding their menagerie of toys up and down the sidewalk. But their favorite thing was to ride in large circles around a large driveway.

The problem: we both had gravel drives—not conducive to smooth rides on bikes, not to mention tricycles and wheeled horses.

The solution: in the house between us lived a wonderful couple who had a smoothly paved drive and welcomed the kids into it anytime. What we moms found amusing was that the kids seemed to think it was *their* driveway and no one else (cars in particular) should use it. One holiday weekend our two youngest had just gotten out several riding toys to haul over to the drive. As we approached, two cars full of out-of-town relatives, who apparently weren't notified of the driveway agreement, pulled in and parked in the middle of the neighbor's drive—one on each side.

The kids looked at the cars, turned and looked at us, then back at the cars. Confused, puzzled, not happy to have lost their “freeway” they headed for the sidewalk. Someone had overstepped into their territory.

Another day the younger two were riding, enjoying trying to run into each other in a kiddie demolition derby, and making it hard for the older ones to avoid them while riding their “big” bikes around.

My neighbor's oldest daughter, five at the time, decided she would make lanes for everyone to drive in. She announced this loudly, and disappeared into the house. A few minutes later she reappeared with a roll of crepe paper streamers and some tape. She proceeded to mark off three lanes with the streamers and then told the "babies" (who were both approaching three years) which lanes they were to use.

The wind was already snapping at the streamers, making the lanes crooked. My youngest son, after having his attention drawn to the streamers, ran over and picked up one end, letting it blow loose in the wind.

The five-year-old "lane boss" immediately descended on him, scolding him about touching "her" lanes. But her younger sister was already headed over to dismantle what was left of the boundary system. She looked at the "babies," huffed, gathered up the blowing streamers, wadded them up and handed them to her mother on the way to play somewhere else!

The boundaries she set were violated before they were even observed. So she gave up and went on to something else.

I'm so grateful God doesn't do that. From the beginning with Eve and Adam in the garden, we as God's creation in his own image have violated the boundaries he sets for us. The Israelites did it over and over. He punished them, yet still cared for them and took care of them. King David committed sins we would find difficult to abide or overcome—adultery, murder—but God knew David's heart and protected him.

With Christ, God set some new boundaries for us, but our nature is the same and even without hundreds of rules to remember, we cross the boundaries and disappoint our loving Father.

Regardless of the boundaries we cross, God's love for us is boundless. *"But because of His great love for us, God, who is rich in mercy, made us alive with Christ even when we were dead in transgressions—it is by grace you have been saved."—Ephesians 2:4-5*

As you seek your 10 minutes' peace this week, remember it can only be found inside the boundaries of Christ's sacrifice and the abundance of God's love. Pray that the boundaries around sin will be clear to us as we seek to turn away from it, and invisible when we do sin and seek to return to our Father.

"Casting Crowns"

When my oldest son was seven we attended a Veteran's Day ceremony at our city park with the Cub Scouts. He was not too sure about what was going on, but was excited to be there as part of an official group.

In our small town the agenda is short and simple. Included each year are women of the VFW Auxiliary laying a wreath at the foot of a statue honoring our fallen men and women of the armed forces.

As the wreath was solemnly placed at the base of the statue, the crowd stood quietly. Then came the twenty-one gun salute and playing of taps.

As I tried to explain to my son what they were doing, another image came to mind. The shape of the wreath became that of a crown. Rather than a statue, I pictured Christ.

Flashback to the previous summer, as I attended a Christ in Youth conference with my youth group. I found myself in the middle of the most moving combination of worship and revival service I have ever witnessed.

These teens, some committed to a lifetime of godly service and some who didn't yet know Christ, were asked to lay their crowns (cardboard ones from Burger King provided by the youth leaders) at the foot of a large cross in the front.

Throughout the evening they were invited to go to one of several stations around the auditorium and commit, confess, cry—whatever they felt was necessary to meet God there.

Hundreds did. Without embarrassment. Many without delay, knowing that everyone in the room supported them and was lifting them up in prayer. (How many of us would feel comfortable doing that in our home congregation?)

Several of the kids from my group still remember that as a pivotal point in their relationship with Christ. For a couple of them, it was the beginning. But for everyone there that night, it was evidence of how the Spirit moves when we cast our crowns before a gracious Savior and give ourselves up wholly to Him.

At least once a year we honor and remember veterans who sacrificed. But we need to be casting our crowns daily before the Lord, thanking Him for his love and grace, seeking to serve and just lifting our hands and voices in praise!

"They lay their crowns before the throne and say: 'You are worthy, our Lord and God, to receive glory and honor and power, for you created all things, and by your will they were created and have their being.' "—Revelation 4:10-11

"Stars & Stripes"

Flags are flying, firecrackers popping, ice cream melting, swimmers splashing—it's that red, white and blue time of year.

Independence Day (or the Fourth of July as we commonly call it—I wonder why?) was always as full of tradition as other holidays in my family. But as we have all grown up and added in-laws and children it's hard to get together and keep up the familiar.

When I was younger we always went to my grandparents home on the farm where we would gorge on watermelon (My grandpa always said the watermelons weren't really ready until July 4th and he could always choose or grow a delicious one!), homemade ice cream—cranked by hand, of course, and homemade cookies. We would set off our own selection of fireworks and watch the big displays which were visible from several area communities right from the back yard.

I never liked the loud fireworks, which of course my brother just had to buy. Many times I found myself in the house after the "pretty" ones were gone. To avoid the noise I would watch "The Music Man," a Fourth of July staple, or the celebration from Washington, D.C. or Boston with the fireworks accompanied by a live orchestra playing "The 1812 Overture."

Some of my traditions sound like sappy cliches, but I guess maybe that's why they became traditions. They may be too tame or lame for some, but I think they represent what Independence Day is about: celebration of a place where we can celebrate in almost any way we choose.

We can gather with those we love. We can pray together. We can eat too much sugar and make too much noise and, for the most part, no one will be bothered by it. I hope my children will not laugh at all the Independence Day traditions I try to keep alive, but more importantly, I hope they wil! acquire a desire to celebrate the traditions of the Lord's Independence day—his death on the cross, bearing our sins. And I hope they will want to celebrate it each week as they remember his death and resurrection in fellowship with others.

If they love the "stars and stripes" I hope it is because they are Christ-followers in a nation founded for those who want to follow Christ. When they look at our beloved flag, may it represent more than those who gave their lives for our country's independence. May it also remind us of the Maker of the stars and His son, who bore cruel stripes that we might have independence from the bonds of sin.

During your 10 minutes this week, thank God for those men and women who have fought with voices, pens and weapons to make this a Christian nation. Ask Him to help us continue that fight, that our nation and the world might know freedom through Him.

"Good Morning, Lord"

I am not a morning person. In fact, rather than greet someone with the phrase, "Good morning," I will say "hello," "how are you?" or any other inane greeting that comes to mind. This doesn't mean I don't think it's good morning for someone. I just haven't been convinced yet.

A friend of mine will often open an event with a prayer of "Good morning, Lord," which is not just a greeting but a praise, a verbal high-five if you will. We are congratulating and thanking God for creating a beautiful day and including us in it. Upon hearing this, I can't help but agree with it and feel that it is a good morning. God has a wonderful, individualized day planned for each of us if we just take time to come to Him and get the schedule.

It's so easy to let our own schedule crowd God out of our thoughts and lives during a busy morning. Then the afternoon gets hectic and we just want to relax in the evening, and we're so tired we really meant to pray before falling asleep, but..

When the morning begins not with an alarm clock but a soggy toddler in your bed and the clothes you had planned to wear have a button missing and you're out of milk *and* Poptarts and the dog gets out of the pen and the car won't start and your picky eater left his lunch box at home...I've had those mornings, thankfully not all at once!

Psalm 118:24 says—quote it with me—*"This is the day the Lord has made, let us rejoice and be glad in it."*—that day includes the morning!

Now there are some of you who can't understand why everyone doesn't bound out of bed at 5:30 a.m. and run two miles, iron everyone's clothes for the day and cook a healthy breakfast for the family. All I can say to you is—snooze alarm!

God created the morning and evening and apparently he created people who like to sleep during both times so there would always be someone awake to enjoy His world. How awesome is that?

In Psalm 5:3 David says, *"In the morning, O Lord, you hear my voice; in the morning I lay my requests before you and wait in expectation."*

Although I'm not always awake and alert each morning, I am alive and I thank God for that. It may be a quick prayer, just an acknowledgment of the day and the opportunities ahead, but I do greet the Lord each morning. How can I not? He greets me majestically each day with sunshine or snowfall, flowering trees or falling leaves, smiling, crying or sometimes even blessedly snoozing children.

Good morning, Lord…

"I'm in Charge"

My son developed a large ego at age three. One day at his grandparents' home he put a bucket on his head (a hat in his mind, I suppose—hey, he's got a weird sense of humor), marched into the living room and told his grandpa, "I'm in charge of the weather!"

Whether he came up with this idea on his own (plausible), or had it put into his head by his big brother or one of his uncles (probable), he was sincere.

He did like to be in charge and was relentless in trying to wear down the grown-ups in the house until he got what he wanted. You know, the type of child where the distraction method doesn't work. We would finally get him to sleep and be convinced he would forget by the time he woke up. But he would open his eyes and immediately begin the same request as before.

It sounds like he is a rude and spoiled child, which I pray he is not. But he is determined to get his way.

Am I that stubborn with God? So many times I think I know what's best and I pray for God to help me do it my way instead of being still before Him to find out what His way might be.

I struggle with this on big and small issues. And I don't even want to be in charge of the weather. I'd be happy just to get an accurate forecast most of the time. (But as we say in Illinois, "If you don't like the weather, wait a minute.")

I know that God is in charge of the weather. My son knows it too, but wouldn't accept it at age three. Perhaps I can learn from him.

When it comes to the storms of my life, the climate of my household, a sunny disposition, I don't always wait for God to send healing rain, or even to calm the storm.

There's a song called "Little Flowers" which talks about how the flowers never worry when the wind and rain come because without it they wouldn't grow. Like those flowers, I can choose to be "down in the dirt," "comin' on up" or "pretty bloomin' good."

So whatever the actual weather, I'll remember to check out Luke 12:27 for a positive forecast!

"Parenting by the Book"

I love to read—almost anything. Especially books and articles which will help me be more organized, efficient, intelligent and fit.

When I was pregnant with my first son, going on and on about what I had read and how careful I was supposed to be, not eating this or doing that, and how complicated breast feeding sounded, my mother told me to stop reading so much!

Years later, in reading some magazine articles on how to understand why children lie, and what toys are the most likely to stimulate their impressionable little brains, I realized I have become a more discerning reader.

I no longer believe everything I read, and even those things I do believe, I realize don't necessarily apply to me. I didn't worry whether I had done everything in the article or even make a note in my organizer to try it out as soon as possible.

I'm not saying I will stop reading parenting magazines or self-help books, but I do try to choose them carefully—searching out what I want to know more about or improve upon, rather than reading it all, then feeling overwhelmed and like I have failed.

There is one book that I will still read and worry about living up to, and that I would recommend as the ultimate parenting guide. Even though it may not address the newest method in potty training or give tips on healthy after-school snacks, the Bible never fails with the basics. And we can make the other stuff up as we go along!

There are many scriptures which are immensely helpful in parenting and teaching our children which do not even relate to those topics. But I want to focus on a few which do directly speak to parents.

Proverbs 17:6 says *"...parents are the pride of their children."* Hmm—seems like our society thinks it's the other way around.

1 Timothy 5:4 says, *"But if a widow has children or grandchildren, these should learn first of all to put their religion into practice by caring for their own family and so repaying their parents and grandparents, for this is pleasing to God."* Our society admonishes us to work and save for our children's education and our own retirement—we wouldn't want to be a burden on anyone, after all.

How about Ephesians 6:4, *"Children, obey your parents in the Lord, for this is right. Honor your father and mother—which is the first commandment with a promise—that it may go well with you and that you may enjoy long life on the earth. Fathers, do not exasperate your children; instead bring them up in the training and instruction of the Lord."*

I don't mention these particular scriptures to say that our plans are wrong or that everyone has lost respect for parents, but to point out that God has a plan for us as parents and He is on our side if we follow that plan.

May God give you wisdom in your choices this week.

"Laughing All the Way"

At two years old, my youngest son discovered money. He liked to get change from his grandpas and carry it around the house. He would bring his offering to Sunday school where there was a bank shaped like a church building. He liked to remove the "roof" and take the money back out, not because he had changed his mind about giving it, but because he enjoyed putting it back in.

For him and for others in his class, giving their money to Jesus was fun!

The phrase, "laughing all the way to the bank" is probably familiar to most of us, but do we have the same attitude when we bank on the Lord? When we return to Him only a portion of what he has blessed us with, knowing we will be blessed in some way by our faith, do we laugh all the way to the offering plate?

Giving should make us feel good, but that's not why we should be giving to God. Nor should it be as a down payment on future riches or "favors" we hope God will see fit to grant us. He doesn't work that way. He doesn't need to because we don't have anything He needs.

When we give, it needs to be from joyful hearts, full of love for God and others, with the purpose and prayer that our money will help others know Him more.

It also requires trust. Trust that God will provide for us and bless us, whether materially, spiritually or in some way we can't imagine. When we give with complete love and trust, the blessings for us and those who benefit from our giving will be bountiful.

That's the warm, fuzzy side of giving.

The practical side necessitates that we plan ahead, know what we can and will give, and have it ready when the offering plate is passed. It's an area where we should ask for God's guidance, and something couples should discuss and come to an agreement on.

These are all difficult things, especially for a young family who may be struggling financially, or an elderly person on a fixed income. But God is God and He is bigger than any situation.

So this week when you prepare your offering or dig out change to send to Sunday school with the kids, take ten minutes to thank God for allowing us to be part of His plan through our giving.

I pray also that I can instill a love for God in my sons, that they might desire to give generously to the Lord of not only their money, but time and talent as well. That they will serve with an unspeakable joy!

"Each man should give what he has decided in his heart to give, not reluctantly or under compulsion, for God loves a cheerful giver. And God is able to make all grace abound to you, so that in all things at all times, having all that you need, you will abound in every good work. As it is written: "He has scattered abroad his gifts to the poor; his righteousness endures forever."—2 Corinthians 9:7-9.

"Comfort and Peace"

One Sunday while sitting in a church service, I became distracted. While trying to listen to the sermon I was captivated by a beautiful, dark-haired baby two rows in front of me.

She had her chin resting on her dad's shoulder and was searching my face, wide-eyed and curious. I smiled at her, but she didn't change her expression and never made a sound.

As her father gently rocked her, she turned her head to the side, snuggled into his shoulder and closed her eyes. She drifted into a comfortable sleep almost instantly.

That's when I realized *I* had been the distraction. As soon as she turned from me and back toward her father, she experienced peaceful sleep.

I felt my heavenly Father pulling me back to the message from His word, and I wondered how many times during the week I am distracted from what my Father has to offer me?

If I can only turn to Him with each distraction, I can find peace and comfort.

Psalm 29:11 says, *"The Lord gives strength to his people, the Lord blesses his people with peace."*

Search for that peace each day this week as you take ten minutes (or more) and shut out the distractions that keep you from your Father.

"Some Things Never Change"

Have you noticed that some things never change?

The smell of corn growing in summer;
Cut grass on a hot day (or a wet, cool one);
The sound of insects through the screened porch;
Sweet watermelon on a hot July evening;
Hugs from people we love;
Summer flying past;
School edging into summer;
The thrill of buying school supplies (without being thrilled about school);
Scents of earth and air and water after a thunderstorm;
God.

He is the same from everlasting to everlasting. He is the Alpha and the Omega—beginning and end. He is God. He is in charge. He loves us. He desires our love.

Aren't you glad some things never change?

"I the Lord do not change."—Malachi 3:6

Reflect this week on things you love which have remained constant in your life. Thank God for them. Tell your children about them, or write down some stories as a keepsake.

"Schoolhouse Wisdom"

Sometimes it's easy to forget that what our kids learn at home gets taken to school with them. We are with them many hours, days, even years before the school system has a chance to mold them.

So why do we worry so much about how school will affect them? Perhaps because we doubt our ability as parents to make a strong impression of right and wrong. Sure, maybe we're confident that they will chew with their mouths closed and say "Please" and "Thank you," but will they make the right decisions when someone bullies them on the playground or offers them drugs in the locker room?

They will if we have prepared them and continue to re-enforce the values we expect of them and the good decisions that they make.

School is really no different from Sunday school, except we are more trusting of the latter. We may take our kids to church and leave them in their class expecting that they will learn biblical truths and values. But unless they are being taught by someone who understands and upholds those values and knows how to communicate them to children of that age, our children may not learn.

As parents, we are ultimately responsible for instilling God's word and every important value in our children. We are blessed if we have a network of Christian teachers at church or in school to help us with the task, but seeing that they get the information is up to us. So is modeling the lifestyle.

For thousands of years God has given His people the task of

passing down his teachings to the next generation. Deuteronomy 11:18-20 says, *"Fix these words of mine in your hearts and minds; tie them as symbols on your hands and bind them on your foreheads. Teach them to your children, talking about them when you sit at home and when you walk along the road, when you lie down and when you get up. Write them on the doorframes of your houses and on your gates."*

Even though our children will hear about and experience many lifestyles when they enter school, whether in kindergarten, junior high, college or the school of the real world, if we have instilled biblical truths in their hearts and modeled a Christ-like lifestyle for them, they will be able to face diversity and conduct themselves appropriately.

For children in a home school or Christian school, this may not be an issue for years to come, but those in public school will face additional challenges and we should be in prayer for them.

Parents with children attending public school also should be informed about the policies of the school and the rights of their children, especially relating to religious expression. Remember that the overwhelming majority of teachers and administrators are there because they care about our children. We may not agree with every decision they make, but we should respect and honor their authority in front of our children.

Though laws vary by state, students are allowed to participate in prayer meetings or groups as an extra-curricular activity as long as they are student-led. There also is no restriction concerning reading a bible at school as long as it is done silently during "free" time.

Again, since laws vary by state, we will want to find out what specifically applies to our children.

As parents we have to remember that the goal is to teach our kids to live Christ. Sometimes battles have to be won along the way, but they shouldn't necessarily become our focus.

Have a blessed school year and help your kids show Christ in the schoolhouse!

As you find your ten minutes this week, pray for all the students going back to school, at every age level. Pray for teachers who will be helping mold them. Pray for administrators and board members who have to make difficult decisions. Pray for support personnel like teacher aides, cooks, secretaries, janitors, bus drivers and all the others who are often overlooked and under-appreciated. Pray that the Holy Spirit will work through Christians in your school district to create a better atmosphere for learning.

"And They're Off..."

Depending on the ages and temperaments of your children, the tears you cry when that school bell rings again may be from joy or sadness. Or they may just be a nostalgic mixture of memories, hopes and prayers.

Technology, politics and violence have transformed the school experience even since I was in school. Chalk has been replaced by allergen-free dry erase markers. Computers may read more books to a child than the teacher. Complex security measures can make entering a grade school feel like trying to get through an international airport.

These things are not bad, just different. They are adaptations to the world we live in—a world that insists we change or be left behind.

Jesus Christ also tells us we must change or be left behind. In John 12:36 He says, *"Whoever serves me must follow me; and where I am my servant also will be."* In 1 Peter 3:11 we are reminded to *"turn from evil and do good; seek peace and pursue it."*

There are many ways our lives can and should change to adapt to the world around us. But our hearts must remain pure, seeking the Lord. This is a difficult balancing act, and is only complicated by the demands of our daily lives.

With the school year comes an entire calendar full of activities: sports, Scouting; church programs; dance and piano lessons—more extra activities than we have time for.

But unless we carve out time for the Lord, for our own study and prayer time as parents, and for family time and church fellowship, all those other activities become meaningless. We can't be at our best, much less a Christ-like example to others, if we don't spend one-on-one time with the Lord.

So as the kids race to school this year and we race into that busy fall schedule, let's focus on the only race that counts—the one that will end with a crown of righteousness because we have run toward God and set the pace and course for others to follow!

"Where's Your Allegiance?"

Watching kindergartners say the Pledge of Allegiance to the flag each morning for several years, I noticed that some were quite intent—eyes fixed firmly on the flag, voices strong, hands placed carefully over their hearts. Others fidgeted, mumbled or looked around, their hands on everything but their hearts. Sometimes one slipped under the radar of the pledge leader and the teachers and didn't even stand up!

What did I learn from watching this display (or non-display) of patriotism? Consistently the kids who stood tall and said the pledge with their hands and eyes in the proper places were the ones who knew how to listen and follow directions in other areas of the class. They also had less trouble getting through the day.

I can relate this to my pledge to Christ—to honor Him, to seek things which are right and good. When I fidget through the sermon on Sunday, mumble a prayer out of obligation, use my hands to fulfill my desires rather than to promote God's kingdom or help those in need, or have my eyes on the things of earth rather than things above, it can be a difficult day!

Sometimes it's hard to keep everything going in the right direction at the same time. (Kind of like patting your head and rubbing your tummy.) But I notice that when I lack in even one area—prayer, fellowship, scripture reading, kindness to others—that my whole relationship with the Lord can slip a notch.

Although I may be busy with many things each day, as most of us are—spouse, children, school, career, sports, church activities, housekeeping, bill paying—and I may make a pledge to the flag, my true and total allegiance was pledged to Christ when I gave my life to Him. I must remember through all the everyday-ness that my allegiance is to Jesus and I must fix my eyes on Him.

"Let us fix our eyes on Jesus, the author and perfecter of our faith, who for the joy set before him endured the cross, scorning its shame, and sat down at the right hand of the throne of God."—Hebrews 12:2

"Seasons"

A kindergarten boy in the class where I work was answering questions for a quarterly progress report. By mid-year the kids are supposed to know the days of the week, the months of the year and seasons.

When he was asked about the four seasons he answered, "Basketball, football, soccer and hockey." I guess we know what the emphasis was at his house!

My favorite season is fall. I love crisp, cool air and falling leaves. My kids love summer so they can be outside for hours each day. We all have our favorite season of the year.

But not many of us, when asked our favorite season, would answer "death" or "mourning" or "financial hardship."

They may not be our favorites, but they are some of the seasons of life. Ecclesiastes 3 tells us there is a season for everything under heaven.

Even though God is a good God and loves us, there will still be unpleasant seasons in our lives. People will get sick and die. Relationships will fall apart. Wars and natural disasters will occur. And God will be there for us through every season.

I would be happy to live where the seasons call for temperatures to top out at seventy-five degrees. However, I have a co-worker who would like it to never get colder than seventy-eight. I used to tease her about wanting some snow days!

Just as we have to survive and even thrive in weather we don't like, we have to do the same spiritually through all seasons of life. We can't do it well, though, without the forecast for eternal life through Christ's blood, the umbrella of God's love, the watertight boots of His Word and a sturdy raincoat of Christian brothers and sisters.

We prepare for the weather most days by watching the forecast, whether we put faith in it or not, and getting out the umbrella, the sun screen or the snow boots to battle the elements. Why then, wouldn't we put even more planning into spiritually preparing for the seasons of life. Study of God's Word, prayer, fellowship, worship—to guard against the elements of the world.

As you meditate on the Word this week, pray that what you study will fortify you for this season.

"Good Enough"

In preschool my son made a magnetic clothespin with an apple attached to the front. It was designed to display his work on the refrigerator. On the front of it was printed, "My work is good enough to eat!"

One day my brother, who was in college at the time, came over and happened to notice it hanging there. He said, "I want one of these that says 'John's work is *good enough*!'" (Quite the comedian.)

Wouldn't we all like to be told at the end of the day that our work is "good enough." Very few people, if any, would feel that way about themselves every day. Some of us could name people we think would fit the description of being good enough in our eyes or even in God's eyes.

But the truth is, none of us is "good enough"! That's why God sent us someone who was—His son Jesus. He was goodness itself, perfect, blameless—something none of us can claim.

When called "Good teacher" by a ruler, Jesus even asked, "Why do you call me good?" He then continued, "No one is good except God alone."

There are many things about us which are good. We can do much good when we work with a godly purpose, but our works and our faith are not "good enough." We need the perfection of Jesus Christ.

Let's celebrate daily the gift God gave of himself to allow us a relationship with Him, even though we can never be "good enough."

"What's Your Name?"

You don't have to go to a foreign country or even a big city to find unusual names. Everyone wants to be unique! Some change their names from the mundane ones they were given at birth to the fabulous ones they always wanted. Others live with the conservative names they were given and then saddle their kids with outrageous names.

One of the hardest things to figure out is the spellings. In the small grade school my son attended there were at least five different spellings of the names Cheyenne and Brittany. (Apparently the parents like the popular name, but still want their child to stand out.)

Celebrities have led the way in recent years with creative and weird baby names. Some include Seven (a girl) and Banjo (a boy). I once worked with a woman whose husband was a district manager for a major soft drink company. He insisted they name their daughter Pepsi Nicola. Her mother called her Nicki.

I always thought my name was unimaginative and old-fashioned, but at least everyone could spell S-U-S-A-N. I wanted my kids to have strong, recognizable names, but I didn't want them to have to share their names with three other kids in the class. They are named for family members, but because the names were interesting and made us think of something or someone positive.

I refused to use family names just to keep them in the family! My family has done that for many decades and some names, in my opinion, need to be put to rest with great-aunt Gertrude! (Just for the record, I don't have a great-aunt Gertrude, but I know better than to use the names of my own aunts!)

Many old-fashioned names are very popular again, including biblical ones. I love Noah, David, Adam, Timothy, Tabitha, Sarah, Hannah and others, but I draw the line at a daughter named Oholibamah or a son named Mahalalel.

We dwell on the meaning of names. My names means graceful lily—whish I've never felt I resemble. So does a name make the person? Some scientists who have studied such things, no doubt with large amounts of tax-funded grants, say they do.

Children are sometimes reminded to live up to their name, or not to do anything to blemish the family name. What about teaching our children to live above their names? Perhaps by giving them another name to aspire to, such as "child of God" or "Christ follower"?

The bible gives us many names for God and Christ. These don't change who He is, they only show us the different characteristics He has and help us to see that He can be the Creator of the universe, the Savior of our souls and the Friend of our hearts.

What can we be for Him? Christians, as they were first called in the church at Antioch; encouragers as Barnabas was; salt and light to the world. So many names for us to try to be worthy of...

During your study time this week, flip through several different books in your bible and see how many names describe a faithful Christ follower. Then focus on one or two and try to live up to them all week.

"Changing Tastes"

I used to hate going shopping with my mother when I was in grade school. I loved picking out new clothes or looking at books and records. (Dating myself there, aren't I?), but when it came time to tag along while she looked at things—BOOORING!

She could spend what seemed like hours looking at and trying on clothes. Boring "mom clothes." Nobody cared if their mom was fashionable, did they? Then she would want to stop and look a things like bedding and cookware or clothes for my brother!

By the time I was in junior high, I would beg to bring a friend along and we'd go off and shop in the fun stores while Mom looked at all that boring stuff.

But about the time I was half-way through college and having to semi-furnish an apartment, those housewares departments, appliance displays and aisles of linens became amazingly appealing.

Now I'm getting a taste of my own medicine as my children roll their eyes and whine if I even slow down at Wal-Mart in any department besides toys and food.

As I thought about this change in taste, I realized I have done the same thing spiritually.

The more the Holy Spirit works in me and the more I study, understand and live God's Word, the more appealing it becomes. It has relevance in my life it didn't have twenty years ago.

I hope that I will continue to grow in my love for God's word, His people and His purpose. I hope I can instill that love in my children, even if it takes a few years to mature.

As for shopping, I try to reserve the linen aisle for solo outings!

"Let the word of Christ richly dwell within you with all wisdom, teaching and admonishing one another with psalms and hymns and spiritual songs, singing with thankfulness in your hearts to God."— Colossians 3:16

"I Don't Understand"

Some things I will never understand. Algebra has eluded me for over twenty years! Thankfully I don't have to comprehend complex equations to get through life. Then there are the things I don't get, but want to understand. Like who really killed JFK and how does one sock in a pair escape the dryer before I open the door?

Many things in the bible are also confusing, but some I want to decipher even though they may not be essential to my relationship with or understanding of the Lord.

I want to know what the earth was like before the flood. Where did the dinosaurs go? I want to know how many Israelites, including women and children, were led out of Egypt. How did the apostles view the female disciples like Mary Magdalene? Was Paul married at one time? Does the number of the beast have an actual significance for us today?

I haven't found definitive answers to any of these questions yet, but I will keep studying these and many more. The search in itself may help enhance my love for Jesus and increase my gratitude toward God for His grace.

I don't believe God meant for us to have all the answers. If so, He would have been more detailed and descriptive. We don't need to know whether Eve picked an apple or a pomegranate or some fruit that no longer exists, or what Jesus looked like or manna tasted like.

We only need to know that God took care of His people in the desert by providing food—and He will take care of us! We can speculate what Jesus might have looked like, but the color of his skin is less important than the color of his blood, which He willingly shed for us.

I don't understand many things God has done, but I understand His love and my commission to share it. Take ten minutes to thank God for your understanding of His grace and ask for deeper understanding of His will in your life.

"In With the Old"

I am a preservationist at heart. I cry at the thought of a historic structure being torn down. I cringe to see old photographs for sale in an antique store or auction. I mean, who could throw out a seventy-year-old picture of Aunt Mildred, even if they never met her?

My home is an odd collection of old sepia photographs, family heirlooms and what I like to think of as antique furniture, but some dealers might call firewood. I want to know my family's history and traditions and record it for my children.

I love the way my grandmother told about her two younger brothers and a cousin building an airplane from scrap wood, putting the youngest of them inside and "flying" him out of the barn loft. That twenty-foot drop must have made quite an impact because the "pilot" became an engineer!

My relatives have told me countless stories of their lives and the lives of those before them whom I never knew. I treasure each tale.

When I drive around my small hometown I see several old houses for sale, a few of which are falling down, and I wish I had the money to restore them.

Why am I so attached to the past? I can't really answer, except to say that I like knowing where I came from and why things are the way they are now. I like to imagine the people who built that house a couple of blocks from mine and understand why no one took care of it over the years, or cares that it might be demolished.

When I understand the history behind something, I can apply it to my life and make it relevant to the way I live. That's why I love reading and understanding scripture, especially the Old Testament, which is so rich and colorful in history and tradition.

Sometimes there is more explanation than we can comprehend, such as the details of the laws in Leviticus. Other times we get the bare facts and have to imagine the details, like the creation and flood in Genesis.

But what is so wonderful about the scripture, Old or New Testament, is that no matter who reads it or tries to apply it, it remains true. The history of the scripture doesn't change. Sometimes it is interpreted differently by different people, but if we really study and research what was written in the original texts, there are no contradictions. None!

These words have been preserved for thousands of years and come through more generations than we can count, yet they are still whole and accurate. Sadly, we don't have many antiques that can survive thousands of years intact and certainly very little historic record which has remained pure for that long.

I love the song "Ancient Words," which describes the value and purity of the scripture and how it has been handed down. Just as I believe it is my duty to pass on family history and tradition to my children, my higher calling is to pass on the "words of life and words of hope" that God has preserved for us.

I pray that I will be a pure preservationist in sharing the Word.

"For what I received I passed on to you as of first importance: that Christ died for our sins according to the Scriptures, that he was buried, that he was raised on the third day according to the Scriptures, and that he appeared to Peter, and then to the Twelve."—1 Corinthians 15:3-5

"Taking Out the Garbage"

Every Thursday morning a large, loud vehicle would lumber down our street and everyone under the age of six would get excited and stare in fascination out the front window as the air brakes brought it to a squeaking-whooshing halt and a guy in a fluorescent T-shirt jumped out and attached a large trash receptacle to the back.

The kids would point and squeal as it was dumped into the truck. Then it was time for a mad dash to the side window to watch the scene repeated at the neighbor's house. (This was often a good time to sneak off for some quiet time. They wouldn't miss me until it turned the corner at the end of the block!)

I got amused at the way my kids reacted to something as mundane and offensive as the garbage truck. It was quite a sight when I had a home day care and five or six children would crowd in front of the window as the truck came down the street.

But I remember once when I misplaced the garbage bill and didn't pay on time. The truck didn't stop, the kids were disappointed and my husband was not thrilled to get out the extra garbage can to store two weeks' worth of trash. So as mundane and loudly annoying as the garbage truck was, we needed it on a regular basis.

Does our excitement over God's grace fade with the years like the elation over the garbage truck as we grow up? I'm afraid it often does.

But what happens if we don't take out our trash regularly by praying, repenting, praising and being in fellowship with other Christians? The result will stink up our lives, and bad habits, resentment, discontent and temptation will bury us.

God doesn't want that garbage of sin in our lives. So even though he hates it, he graciously and lovingly gave us His son to pick up the trash and put it where neither He nor we have to look at it or be offended by it. (Psalm 103:12)

In 2 Corinthians 2:15-16 Paul says, *"For we are to God the aroma of Christ among those who are being saved and those who are perishing. To the one we are the smell of death; to the other the fragrance of life."*

We know the aroma of Christ is pleasing and pure, not tainted by any of the garbage of sin, and we need others to notice that aroma as well. So when you hear that truck coming this week, reflect on whether you've taken out the spiritual garbage for the day.

"My Best Friend, God"

Parenting experts tell us that we shouldn't be friends with our kids. We can't be the authority figure and the loving disciplinarian as well as someone they pal around with.

I have to agree with that for the most part. Friendship, perhaps, can come later when they have grown up and even become parents themselves.

But there's an exception to this rule—God.

I read a wonderful devotion several years ago about God wanting to be our friend. This wasn't a new concept for me, but thinking of Him in the many different roles at once was rather daunting.

He is our Father, Savior, Creator, Judge, Provider, Protector, and yes, even Friend.

Like any friendship, one with God takes time and effort. We must spend time with Him through prayer and study. We must live a life in which He can comfortably be present. We must be proud to introduce Him to our other friends.

James 2:23 says, *"Abraham believed God, and it was credited to him as righteousness, and he was called God's friend."*

Speaking to his disciples in John 15, Jesus said, *"I no longer call you servants, because a servant does not know his master's business. Instead, I have called you friends, for everything I have learned from my Father, I have made known to you."*

What better friend could we have than one who knew us before time, knows the length of our time, has a plan for how we should spend our time, and spent time as one of us.

Many hymns and praises talk about Jesus as a friend, but I can't think of any that refer to God in that light.

Besides, isn't Jesus as a friend the same as God as a friend? Perhaps. We can picture Jesus as a friend because He took human form. God the Son took human form. God the Creator wants to have a friendship with us. That simplifies things, doesn't it?

We think of God in many of his other roles, but the friend part is hard to grasp. Yet we need to reach for a friendship with our Creator. He's the best friend we can ever have!

"Have a Nice Day"

When I was in high school I worked at a fast food restaurant where we were programmed to end each transaction with "Have a nice day!" One Christmas Eve an older couple came in and ordered coffee. It was obvious the woman had been crying.

As she went to sit down, her husband explained, "We just got a call that our son-in-law was killed in an accident." I'm sure I mumbled something about how sorry I was, but as I served the coffee and handed him the change, that reflex kicked in and out of my mouth came THOSE WORDS, "Have a nice evening." (Yeah, right.)

Before I finished speaking the words, I knew they were stupid, even callous. Many times since I have wished I'd said, "Have a safe trip" or "You'll be in my prayers."

Although unintentional, the words were insensitive. How many times have I unintentionally said something which hurt someone?

I can think of several instances where I have said something to an individual or in a group setting and then stewed for hours or days over whether one person may have misinterpreted what I said or taken it as an insult. Sometimes I have even called that person and gone over my concern with them to be sure there are no hurt feelings or misunderstandings.

I strive to seek God's guidance in my words and to be conscientious of what the other person is feeling before I speak. I want my words to encourage others and lift them up, or at the very least not discourage.

As you take your ten minutes this week, ask God to reveal to you any hurtful words you may have spoken and to order your words each time you open your mouth. One of my favorite T-shirt slogans is "Lord, put your arm around my shoulder and your hand over my mouth!"

Amen!

"Pleasant words are a honeycomb, sweet to the soul and healing to the bones."—Proverbs 16:24

"I Can Do It Myself"

When our youngest son was about two he was dubbed the "mountain goat," among other names. He thought he could and should climb everything—and he did! No matter the obstacle, he found a way to scale it.

Mostly the climbing was the result of wanting to be independent. Unfortunately, this sometimes had a bad outcome.

He hoisted himself up on the bathroom counter to reach his toothbrush in the cabinet, usually bumping his head on the door. He scaled the piano top (no pun intended) to put loose change in the bank, but stepped on the keys in the process. He even learned to climb over the gate at the top of the stairs—going down! I expected one day to find him on top of the refrigerator or playing with the squirrels in a nearby tree.

Usually when he was told to stop climbing and wait for help, he ignored the voice and would strike out on his own only to end up falling off or breaking something.

I wonder if God ever wants to tell me, "Hey! Just wait a minute and I'll help you get that. You can't quite do that on your own, but if you let me help you can reach it safely."

God provides me with so many stepping stones—His Word, prayer, other Christians to encourage and lift me up. But I still need Him. Sometimes a situation requires a boost from the Divine.

The weekly schedule I have packed so full of practices and services and things that have to be done, but barely left time for a quick prayer or quiet devotion, may become a jumbled mess simply because I was sure I could do everything myself.

After all, I am a wife and mother and could claim many other titles as well. I'm capable of handling the day to day. Aren't I? Perhaps I left out my most important title—child of God. To claim that one I have to let Him be the parent.

We probably are all familiar with Psalm 121:1,*"I lift up my eyes to the hills. Where does my help come from? My help comes from the Lord, the Maker of heaven and earth."*

He's the creator of the universe and he doesn't even need a day planner! I think he can handle those little obstacles I see as mountains.

Psalm 30:2 says, *"O Lord my God, I called to you for help and you healed me."* and in 18:6 it says, *"In my distress I called to the Lord; I cried to my God for help. From his temple he heard my voice; my cry came before him, into his ears."*

I have to remember that God wants to help me in the good times as well, when, shamefully, I may not take time to come to him for guidance. In Psalm 20 David says, *"May (the Lord) give you the desire of your heart and make all your plans succeed... May the Lord grant all your requests."*

David knew about asking the Lord, getting the desires of his heart and what happened when he didn't wait for God's way.

As you seek peaceful time this week, wait on the Lord. Ask Him for help in reaching the desires of your heart. He is a loving Father. He will listen.

"Thanks a Lot"

I know I don't thank people nearly enough. I'm not timely with thank-you notes the way my mother taught me to be. In fact, if the phrase "thanks a lot" comes out of my mouth, it is likely to be sarcastic.

The thankful season is upon us. (Should it ever be out of season?) We are encouraged to pause and thank God and others for the blessings in our lives.

Despite my sarcasm and tendency to see the negative side of things, I am thankful and express that to God daily. But living it is a harder thing to do.

So during this "thankful season" I remind myself to thank others, to live like I believe God's promises and to acknowledge the thanks and blessings of other people.

There are too many scriptures for me to begin listing the "thanks" of those whose examples we should follow. Take a few minutes as you digest that food you are so thankful for and look up a few favorites. Share them with your children or with family members who don't know the Lord.

Even if they don't thank you, you'll be blessed.

"Good Reporting"

Answer the five "W's"—who, what, when, where and why. That's the rudimentary formula for good reporting. Then you learn to snag the audience with buzz words and catch phrases, attempting to be fair and accurate and fitting it all into the allotted space. (Which is usually about two columns shorter than you need.)

These are just a few of the lessons I learned in journalism school. I also learned how to meet deadlines and deal with massive quantities of stress. I did not master drinking coffee or smoking, which I was told is a must to be a successful journalist. Perhaps that's why I'm writing devotionals instead of hard-hitting news.

Anyway, the point I'm trying to get to is that I was taught to seek the reason behind things and give details when possible, especially in feature stories, where the details are what holds the reader's attention. I also have a natural inquisitiveness (my husband calls it being nosy) that compels me to seek the deeper meaning, root cause or background of a story. And I want a follow-up!

So when I read the bible, sometimes I wonder why God didn't give us more information. Many things can be better understood by studying the cultural setting of the time. Some can be answered with archeology or science. But many will never be resolved. At least not in this life.

When I read the gospels, I prefer Luke because he's methodical and chronological. It makes more sense to me. Maybe he was a journalist at heart and his parents pushed him into a medical career.

I realize that God chose the writers of the bible for a purpose. He inspired them to impart to us what He wanted us to know. His purpose was to give us truth, not to answer every question that anyone through time might possibly have about whether Adam rode dinosaurs or what type of fruit was on the tree in Eden.

Never mind where Many Magdalene got her money or how many brothers and sisters Jesus had or what the color "pale" really is.

But I want details!

The fact that many bible accounts are non-specific or downright vague has intrigued me to study more about the culture and customs of the people. I have ready many scholars' ideas and theories. I have begun to realize that the bible can be much more intensely personal because we can each seek to discover or imagine these details for ourselves.

By this I don't mean making up stories or adding things that didn't happen, but researching what things might have been like, picturing how they happened, understanding what the original language said, while always praying for wisdom and insight.

That's good reporting!

"You statutes are wonderful; therefore I obey them. The unfolding of your words gives light; it gives understanding to the simple."— Psalm 119:129-130

"Biblical Stress Busters"

Stress relief for the holidays, or anytime.

*With a cup of herbal tea (and even a friend)—Read Psalm 37.

*While listening to Christmas music (Point of Grace is awesome, as is any Celtic instrumental)—Read 24 (or any chapter in Isaiah).

*While eating something decadent and chocolate—Read Proverbs 12

*Soaking in a tub of hot water and sweet-smelling bubbles (with the bathroom door *locked*)—Read Psalm 62.

*Driving to a holiday celebration or performance (along with your fellow travelers)—Pray for those involved in the celebration, that God will be glorified through what happens and someone who needs to hear about Christ will have listening ears.

*Enjoying the lights on your Christmas tree (with your spouse)—Read by candlelight Song of Solomon 1.

*While doing holiday baking (or to force yourself to do some holiday baking)—Listen to upbeat Christmas music and dance (I recommend Jaci Velasquez and Harry Connick Jr.).

*After watching "It's a Wonderful Life" with your family—Read Psalm 139 together.

* While wrapping gifts—Wrap up something you have on hand or make a mental list of people to whom you could give small or homemade gifts. Focus on those who may not have much family or who need to see Christ's love.

*Make an unexpected visit—Drop in on a friend or neighbor you don't often see and bring them some tea or hot chocolate mix or a Christmas ornament. Find out how they are doing and let them know you are praying for them. Keep it short.

*Tucking your kids into bed the week before Christmas—Read them Luke 1 & 2

Keep yourself in the Word during this busy time, stay connected to your Father and try a few of these ideas for a quick pick-me-up. They don't take much time, money or planning!

"Simple Beauty"

My kids love to look at Christmas lights. The neighbor's house with blue lights lining the roof and candy canes in the yard used to elicit much pointing and yelling, "Look, look!" from my sons.

We've seen some spectacular displays over the years. From parks with every fairy tale and cartoon you can think of cut out in cardboard, painted and lighted with a rainbow of colors, to the living, working village of Bethlehem, complete with armed Roman soldiers who arrested and jailed unsuspecting members of the group. (Including a few junior high boys…hmm.)

But one December night I saw a display which made a bigger impression than all those fancy light shows and realistic portrayals.

As we were driving along a rural highway we passed an old farm. It had a cozy-looking, two-story farm house and a sturdy old barn, along with some smaller outbuildings. This was not a pretentious place, just very stereotypical.

On the side of the barn, which had probably stood guard along the road for a century, was a cross laid out in white lights. It reached from the peak of the hayloft to the ground.

There were no other Christmas lights or visible holiday decorations on the entire place. Nothing twinkled, no colors flashed. Santa and his reindeer weren't about to go airborne off the rooftop.

There wasn't even a "Merry Christmas" sign or a Christmas tree to be seen through the window.

The simplicity of this holiday display shook me. What a witness to the reason for the season!

Just a simple cross—but it's so much more to those of us who know the story of a tiny baby, grown to be a man, who went willingly to a much rougher, uglier cross and bled for someone like me who can't even make it through the day, much less the season, without complaining how far behind I am and how I still have so much decorating and shopping to do.

This week I hope you will join me in focusing on the simple beauty of the cross, the star, the stable—any one aspect of the Christ story which brings you peace and puts you in a frame of mind to spread the true spirit of Christmas.

"Lego Jesus"

At Christmas time we see decorations of every size, shape and color. Not only fun holiday items like Santa and Christmas trees, but even nativity scenes get tweaked a bit.

Most of us have a little porcelain or wooden nativity set we put in a place of honor each year. The kids may have their own set, made of stuffed people and animals or resin, or even plastic ones modeled after cartoon characters or animals.

We have a church in our town which portrays a living nativity. I love seeing what it might have been like for Jesus to come into the world. And I have much admiration for Mary, who gave birth under harsh conditions, as did most women of that time.

But I heard some radio personalities talking one holiday season about a display featuring a Lego nativity scene. Yes—Joseph, Mary and Jesus in plastic blocks!

I don't know if it was in miniature, life-sized or somewhere in between. I just know it made me laugh a little. Does this mean I don't have reverence for God's gift of the Christ child and that I've become desensitized to the true meaning of Christmas? I hope not.

What it made me think was that some creative person was using the artistic talent God granted to express something which was important in life—Christ's birth. Whoever created it could just as easily have made a Christmas tree or Santa and the reindeer gang, but instead chose to depict baby Jesus.

Why in Legos? Who knows. Maybe it's a medium that will speak to people who would ignore the live animals or the manger made of white lights. There are those who take Legos quite seriously, even companies who have paid tens of thousands of dollars for the construction of Lego desks in order to recruit top employees for whom this was still a favorite, albeit quirky, past time.

Perhaps the Lego Jesus could touch the imagination and then the heart of one of those future CEOs. What a way to use a gift!

So if you happen to see baby Jesus made from red and blue snap blocks, don't be too offended. Remember, God gave us each a different gift with the intention that we would share His story.

"Little People"

When I was in grade school my brother and I had a house and a school bus from Fisher-Price filled with what we called "Little People." (I don't know their official name.)

Later we added a farm, parking garage, a camper, a castle and Sesame Street to the collection. My best friend from grade school even had a real "Little People" McDonald's with food trays and a drive-thru. I'm still jealous!

In case you haven't figured out what I'm talking about, they were little wooden (later, plastic) people with painted faces and molded plastic hair or hats. They were not as big around as a spool of thread and could be hidden almost anywhere. They had no arms or legs, but for some reason we didn't think that was weird.

We still have most of these sets from our childhood. Some of the braids on the girls have been bitten off and the foam "mattresses" on the beds from the house were long ago peeled away, but overall they are still in great shape and my kids love to play with them.

We have a couple of the newer versions at home. My sons have a village, complete with a pet grooming shop, fast food restaurant and car wash. But they don't play with it nearly as much as they play with my old sets when they visit Granny's house.

Little wonder. (Pun intended.) The new ones are much bigger around. They are all one molded piece and are made of soft plastic, not the tough stuff of the older ones. You couldn't even put teeth marks in those—my brother tried many times! The new larger size is because the old ones were a choking hazard, I guess. (Gasp! My children are still playing with them.)

The new ones also have light plastic cars and trucks which lose their wheels easily. All our old tractors and trucks are still intact. And the old farm animals were jointed. They could run or lie down or bend to eat. The new ones, again, one molded piece of plastic. They have to hop everywhere and sleep standing up.

Why does any of this matter and what could it possibly have to do with a relationship with God? I have no idea! (Just kidding.)

New and improved isn't always an improvement. The older toys have much more character and are more durable, and I don't think any of us ever got one caught in our throats!

God's ways and words are the same. We can seek to understand them in our own life, but they can't be improved upon. God knew how we would be living and what we would be able to comprehend long before any of us took our first breath.

He gave us a book of timeless wisdom and if we get choked on the words it's because we didn't chew them long enough or wash them down with Living Water. His ways have endured fires and famines, dictators and domains, and been around not decades, but millenniums.

There are many alternatives, imitations and new-and-improved versions out there, but his book is still on the best-seller list. We turn to it and return to it because it is familiar and comfortable and we know it to be true!

"All your words are true; all your righteous laws are eternal."— Psalm 119:160

Printed in the United States
47667LVS00002B/64-270

9 781424 120451